Second Grade Workbook

Multiplication & Division Skills

BABY PROFESSOR
EDUCATION KIDS

Speedy Publishing LLC
40 E. Main St. #1156
Newark, DE 19711
www.speedypublishing.com

MULTIPLICATION

1. $3 \times 6 =$ _____

2. $2 \times 8 =$ _____

3. $2 \times 12 =$ _____

4. $3 \times 2 =$ _____

5. $3 \times 7 =$ _____

6. $2 \times 4 =$ _____

7. $2 \times 5 =$ _____

8. $2 \times 10 =$ _____

9. $3 \times 3 =$ _____

10. $3 \times 1 =$ _____

11. $3 \times 10 =$ _____

12. $3 \times 8 =$ _____

13. $2 \times 1 =$ _____

14. $2 \times 9 =$ _____

15. $2 \times 11 =$ _______

16. $2 \times 6 =$ _______

17. $3 \times 4 =$ _______

18. $2 \times 2 =$ _______

19. $3 \times 11 =$ _______

20. $3 \times 12 =$ _______

21. $10 \times 12 =$ _______

22. $10 \times 10 =$ _______

23. $5 \times 1 =$ _______

24. $5 \times 12 =$ _______

25. $5 \times 5 =$ _______

26. $5 \times 2 =$ _______

27. $10 \times 1 =$ _______

28. $5 \times 3 =$ _______

29. $5 \times 8 =$ _______

30. $10 \times 4 =$ _______

31. $5 \times 6 =$ _______

32. $10 \times 11 =$ _______

33. 10 × 3 = _______

34. 10 × 6 = _______

35. 10 × 7 = _______

36. 5 × 4 = _______

37. 10 × 2 = _______

38. 5 × 7 = _______

39. 5 × 9 = _______

40. 5 × 10 = _______

41. 2 × 1 = _______

42. 3 × 9 = _______

43. 2 × 4 = _______

44. 2 × 10 = _______

45. 2 × 12 = _______

46. 2 × 2 = _______

47. 3 × 4 = _______

48. 3 × 7 = _______

49. 2 × 7 = _______

50. 3 × 3 = _______

51. $2 \times 11 = $ _______

52. $3 \times 2 = $ _______

53. $3 \times 11 = $ _______

54. $3 \times 1 = $ _______

55. $2 \times 8 = $ _______

56. $3 \times 8 = $ _______

57. $3 \times 6 = $ _______

58. $3 \times 10 = $ _______

59. $3 \times 5 = $ _______

60. $2 \times 6 = $ _______

61. $10 \times 2 = $ _______

62. $10 \times 3 = $ _______

63. $5 \times 2 = $ _______

64. $10 \times 9 = $ _______

65. $5 \times 8 = $ _______

66. $5 \times 11 = $ _______

67. $10 \times 6 = $ _______

68. $5 \times 12 = $ _______

69. 5 × 6 = _______

70. 5 × 3 = _______

71. 5 × 9 = _______

72. 10 × 1 = _______

73. 10 × 11 = _______

74. 10 × 7 = _______

75. 5 × 4 = _______

76. 5 × 7 = _______

77. 5 × 1 = _______

78. 10 × 5 = _______

79. 5 × 10 = _______

80. 5 × 5 = _______

81. 2 × 4 = _______

82. 2 × 3 = _______

83. 3 × 11 = _______

84. 3 × 10 = _______

85. 3 × 8 = _______

86. 2 × 6 = _______

87. $2 \times 5 =$ _______

88. $2 \times 12 =$ _______

89. $3 \times 12 =$ _______

90. $3 \times 4 =$ _______

91. $3 \times 3 =$ _______

92. $2 \times 9 =$ _______

93. $2 \times 8 =$ _______

94. $2 \times 10 =$ _______

95. $3 \times 6 =$ _______

96. $3 \times 1 =$ _______

97. $3 \times 5 =$ _______

98. $2 \times 1 =$ _______

99. $3 \times 7 =$ _______

100. $2 \times 7 =$ _______

101. $10 \times 5 =$ _______

102. $10 \times 7 =$ _______

103. $5 \times 1 =$ _______

104. $5 \times 4 =$ _______

105. 10 × 4 = _______

106. 5 × 5 = _______

107. 10 × 6 = _______

108. 10 × 10 = _______

109. 5 × 11 = _______

110. 5 × 3 = _______

111. 10 × 9 = _______

112. 5 × 9 = _______

113. 10 × 11 = _______

114. 10 × 3 = _______

115. 10 × 2 = _______

116. 5 × 7 = _______

117. 5 × 6 = _______

118. 10 × 1 = _______

119. 5 × 8 = _______

120. 5 × 12 = _______

MISSING FACTOR

1. _______ × 8 = 40

2. 10 × _______ = 80

3. 7 × _______ = 70

4. 3 × _______ = 30

5. 8 × _______ = 80

6. 6 × _______ = 30

7. 2 × _______ = 6

8. _______ × 3 = 6

9. _______ × 7 = 35

10. _______ × 5 = 10

11. 2 × _______ = 4

12. 1 × _______ = 10

13. _______ × 4 = 20

14. 10 × _______ = 50

51. 6 × _______ = 12

52. _______ × 5 = 40

53. 4 × _______ = 40

54. _______ × 4 = 20

55. 7 × _______ = 14

56. 2 × _______ = 10

57. _______ × 5 = 30

58. 10 × _______ = 10

59. 9 × _______ = 45

60. _______ × 10 = 20

61. _______ × 10 = 20

62. _______ × 2 = 16

63. 2 × _______ = 8

64. _______ × 10 = 60

65. 5 × _______ = 35

66. _______ × 8 = 80

67. 8 × _______ = 80

68. _______ × 10 = 40

69. $4 \times$ _______ $= 40$

70. $3 \times$ _______ $= 30$

71. _______ $\times 2 = 12$

72. _______ $\times 6 = 60$

73. _______ $\times 10 = 10$

74. _______ $\times 4 = 8$

75. $2 \times$ _______ $= 10$

76. $4 \times$ _______ $= 8$

77. _______ $\times 2 = 20$

78. $7 \times$ _______ $= 14$

79. _______ $\times 2 = 10$

80. _______ $\times 9 = 90$

DIVISION

1. $15 \div 5 =$ _____

2. $5 \div 1 =$ _____

3. $7 \div 7 =$ _____

4. $8 \div 8 =$ _____

5. $90 \div 9 =$ _____

6. $6 \div 3 =$ _____

7. $32 \div 4 =$ _____

8. $42 \div 7 =$ _____

9. $16 \div 8 =$ _____

10. $4 \div 2 =$ _____

11. $70 \div 7 =$ _____

12. $20 \div 10 =$ _____

13. $36 \div 4 =$ _____

14. $9 \div 9 =$ _____

15. $2 \div 1 =$ _______

16. $7 \div 1 =$ _______

17. $24 \div 4 =$ _______

18. $4 \div 1 =$ _______

19. $60 \div 10 =$ _______

20. $56 \div 7 =$ _______

21. $30 \div 3 =$ _______

22. $6 \div 6 =$ _______

23. $3 \div 3 =$ _______

24. $9 \div 1 =$ _______

25. $20 \div 4 =$ _______

26. $21 \div 3 =$ _______

27. $45 \div 9 =$ _______

28. $20 \div 2 =$ _______

29. $80 \div 10 =$ _______

30. $14 \div 7 =$ _______

31. $45 \div 5 =$ _______

32. $16 \div 8 =$ _______

33. $9 \div 9 =$ _______

34. $12 \div 2 =$ _______

35. $80 \div 8 =$ _______

36. $24 \div 6 =$ _______

37. $18 \div 3 =$ _______

38. $9 \div 3 =$ _______

39. $90 \div 9 =$ _______

40. $10 \div 1 =$ _______

41. $4 \div 1 =$ _______

42. $1 \div 1 =$ _______

43. $18 \div 6 =$ _______

44. $5 \div 1 =$ _______

45. $40 \div 8 =$ _______

46. $48 \div 8 =$ _______

47. $25 \div 5 =$ _______

48. $6 \div 2 =$ _______

49. $8 \div 1 =$ _______

50. $14 \div 2 =$ _______

51. 40 ÷ 5 = _______

52. 40 ÷ 10 = _______

53. 8 ÷ 4 = _______

54. 54 ÷ 6 = _______

55. 21 ÷ 7 = _______

56. 7 ÷ 7 = _______

57. 35 ÷ 7 = _______

58. 4 ÷ 2 = _______

59. 70 ÷ 7 = _______

60. 6 ÷ 1 = _______

61. 14 ÷ 2 = _______

62. 12 ÷ 4 = _______

63. 20 ÷ 4 = _______

64. 56 ÷ 8 = _______

65. 45 ÷ 5 = _______

66. 18 ÷ 9 = _______

67. 21 ÷ 3 = _______

68. 4 ÷ 4 = _______

69. $12 \div 3 =$ _______

70. $18 \div 3 =$ _______

71. $54 \div 6 =$ _______

72. $10 \div 1 =$ _______

73. $40 \div 10 =$ _______

74. $12 \div 6 =$ _______

75. $50 \div 10 =$ _______

76. $48 \div 8 =$ _______

77. $15 \div 3 =$ _______

78. $36 \div 4 =$ _______

79. $8 \div 2 =$ _______

80. $32 \div 4 =$ _______

81. $14 \div 7 =$ _______

82. $54 \div 9 =$ _______

83. $50 \div 5 =$ _______

84. $56 \div 7 =$ _______

85. $20 \div 5 =$ _______

86. $8 \div 1 =$ _______

87. $3 \div 3 =$ _______

88. $27 \div 9 =$ _______

89. $90 \div 9 =$ _______

90. $80 \div 8 =$ _______

91. $45 \div 5 =$ _______

92. $16 \div 4 =$ _______

93. $21 \div 7 =$ _______

94. $28 \div 7 =$ _______

95. $54 \div 6 =$ _______

96. $64 \div 8 =$ _______

97. $36 \div 6 =$ _______

98. $30 \div 5 =$ _______

99. $9 \div 9 =$ _______

100. $80 \div 10 =$ _______

101. $36 \div 9 =$ _______

102. $10 \div 5 =$ _______

103. $12 \div 4 =$ _______

104. $42 \div 6 =$ _______

105. 18 ÷ 6 = ______

106. 18 ÷ 3 = ______

107. 24 ÷ 8 = ______

108. 10 ÷ 2 = ______

109. 6 ÷ 6 = ______

110. 5 ÷ 1 = ______

111. 4 ÷ 1 = ______

112. 30 ÷ 3 = ______

113. 18 ÷ 2 = ______

114. 20 ÷ 2 = ______

115. 63 ÷ 7 = ______

116. 16 ÷ 8 = ______

117. 60 ÷ 6 = ______

118. 90 ÷ 9 = ______

119. 100 ÷ 10 = ______

120. 7 ÷ 7 = ______

MISSING DIVIDEND/ DIVISOR

1. _____ ÷ 6 = 10

2. _____ ÷ 9 = 8

3. 24 ÷ _____ = 3

4. _____ ÷ 9 = 2

5. 20 ÷ _____ = 10

6. 100 ÷ _____ = 10

7. _____ ÷ 2 = 2

8. _____ ÷ 4 = 4

9. _____ ÷ 9 = 9

10. 4 ÷ _____ = 1

11. 10 ÷ _____ = 5

12. 48 ÷ _____ = 8

13. _______ ÷ 6 = 7

14. _______ ÷ 4 = 9

15. _______ ÷ 7 = 8

16. 45 ÷ _______ = 9

17. 80 ÷ _______ = 8

18. 25 ÷ _______ = 5

19. 60 ÷ _______ = 6

20. 16 ÷ _______ = 4

21. 27 ÷ _______ = 9

22. 24 ÷ _______ = 4

23. _______ ÷ 3 = 3

24. 6 ÷ _______ = 1

25. _______ ÷ 9 = 8

26. 14 ÷ _______ = 2

27. 24 ÷ _______ = 3

28. 30 ÷ _______ = 10

29. 100 ÷ _______ = 10

30. 36 ÷ _______ = 4

31. _____ ÷ 2 = 8

32. 36 ÷ _____ = 9

33. _____ ÷ 10 = 10

34. _____ ÷ 3 = 10

35. _____ ÷ 10 = 7

36. _____ ÷ 9 = 2

37. _____ ÷ 8 = 10

38. 40 ÷ _____ = 4

39. _____ ÷ 4 = 2

40. _____ ÷ 4 = 4

41. 30 ÷ _____ = 6

42. 14 ÷ _____ = 7

43. _____ ÷ 10 = 4

44. 30 ÷ _____ = 3

45. 56 ÷ _____ = 8

46. _____ ÷ 2 = 9

47. 24 ÷ _____ = 4

48. _____ ÷ 5 = 10

49. _______ ÷ 2 = 5

50. _______ ÷ 10 = 9

51. 90 ÷ _______ = 10

52. _______ ÷ 6 = 9

53. 54 ÷ _______ = 6

54. _______ ÷ 4 = 10

55. _______ ÷ 10 = 10

56. _______ ÷ 7 = 9

57. 90 ÷ _______ = 9

58. _______ ÷ 8 = 5

59. _______ ÷ 8 = 1

60. _______ ÷ 3 = 9

61. 63 ÷ _______ = 9

62. _______ ÷ 10 = 5

63. _______ ÷ 4 = 3

64. 6 ÷ _______ = 2

65. _______ ÷ 2 = 5

66. _______ ÷ 6 = 2

67. $12 \div \underline{\hspace{2em}} = 2$

68. $30 \div \underline{\hspace{2em}} = 10$

69. $12 \div \underline{\hspace{2em}} = 3$

70. $\underline{\hspace{2em}} \div 2 = 10$

71. $\underline{\hspace{2em}} \div 5 = 2$

72. $\underline{\hspace{2em}} \div 2 = 6$

73. $40 \div \underline{\hspace{2em}} = 8$

74. $\underline{\hspace{2em}} \div 10 = 8$

75. $20 \div \underline{\hspace{2em}} = 10$

76. $\underline{\hspace{2em}} \div 9 = 6$

77. $\underline{\hspace{2em}} \div 10 = 4$

78. $25 \div \underline{\hspace{2em}} = 5$

79. $\underline{\hspace{2em}} \div 8 = 8$

80. $\underline{\hspace{2em}} \div 3 = 1$

MULTIPLICATION

#	Answer		#	Answer		#	Answer
1.	18		30.	40		59.	15
2.	16		31.	30		60.	12
3.	24		32.	110		61.	20
4.	6		33.	30		62.	30
5.	21		34.	60		63.	10
6.	8		35.	70		64.	90
7.	10		36.	20		65.	40
8.	20		37.	20		66.	55
9.	9		38.	35		67.	60
10.	3		39.	45		68.	60
11.	30		40.	50		69.	30
12.	24		41.	2		70.	15
13.	2		42.	27		71.	45
14.	18		43.	8		72.	10
15.	22		44.	20		73.	110
16.	12		45.	24		74.	70
17.	12		46.	4		75.	20
18.	4		47.	12		76.	35
19.	33		48.	21		77.	5
20.	36		49.	14		78.	50
21.	120		50.	9		79.	50
22.	100		51.	22		80.	25
23.	5		52.	6		81.	8
24.	60		53.	33		82.	6
25.	25		54.	3		83.	33
26.	10		55.	16		84.	30
27.	10		56.	24		85.	24
28.	15		57.	18		86.	12
29.	40		58.	30		87.	10

88.	24	99.	21	110.	15
89.	36	100.	14	111.	90
90.	12	101.	50	112.	45
91.	9	102.	70	113.	110
92.	18	103.	5	114.	30
93.	16	104.	20	115.	20
94.	20	105.	40	116.	35
95.	18	106.	25	117.	30
96.	3	107.	60	118.	10
97.	15	108.	100	119.	40
98.	2	109.	55	120.	60

MISSING FACTOR

1.	5	16.	2	31.	9
2.	8	17.	3	32.	5
3.	10	18.	10	33.	5
4.	10	19.	1	34.	2
5.	10	20.	5	35.	4
6.	5	21.	2	36.	7
7.	3	22.	5	37.	10
8.	2	23.	3	38.	3
9.	5	24.	5	39.	5
10.	2	25.	5	40.	5
11.	2	26.	2	41.	5
12.	10	27.	9	42.	5
13.	5	28.	2	43.	5
14.	5	29.	5	44.	5
15.	3	30.	10	45.	3

46.	10	58.	1	70.	10
47.	10	59.	5	71.	6
48.	9	60.	2	72.	10
49.	10	61.	2	73.	1
50.	2	62.	8	74.	2
51.	2	63.	4	75.	5
52.	8	64.	6	76.	2
53.	10	65.	7	77.	10
54.	5	66.	10	78.	2
55.	2	67.	10	79.	5
56.	5	68.	4	80.	10
57.	6	69.	10		

DIVISION

1.	3	15.	2	29.	8
2.	5	16.	7	30.	2
3.	1	17.	6	31.	9
4.	1	18.	4	32.	2
5.	10	19.	6	33.	1
6.	2	20.	8	34.	6
7.	8	21.	10	35.	10
8.	6	22.	1	36.	4
9.	2	23.	1	37.	6
10.	2	24.	9	38.	3
11.	10	25.	5	39.	10
12.	2	26.	7	40.	10
13.	9	27.	5	41.	4
14.	1	28.	10	42.	1

43.	3	**69.**	4	**95.**	9
44.	5	**70.**	6	**96.**	8
45.	5	**71.**	9	**97.**	6
46.	6	**72.**	10	**98.**	6
47.	5	**73.**	4	**99.**	1
48.	3	**74.**	2	**100.**	8
49.	8	**75.**	5	**101.**	4
50.	7	**76.**	6	**102.**	2
51.	8	**77.**	5	**103.**	3
52.	4	**78.**	9	**104.**	7
53.	2	**79.**	4	**105.**	3
54.	9	**80.**	8	**106.**	6
55.	3	**81.**	2	**107.**	3
56.	1	**82.**	6	**108.**	5
57.	5	**83.**	10	**109.**	1
58.	2	**84.**	8	**110.**	5
59.	10	**85.**	4	**111.**	4
60.	6	**86.**	8	**112.**	10
61.	7	**87.**	1	**113.**	9
62.	3	**88.**	3	**114.**	10
63.	5	**89.**	10	**115.**	9
64.	7	**90.**	10	**116.**	2
65.	9	**91.**	9	**117.**	10
66.	2	**92.**	4	**118.**	10
67.	7	**93.**	3	**119.**	10
68.	1	**94.**	4	**120.**	1

1.	60	28.	3	55.	100
2.	72	29.	10	56.	63
3.	8	30.	9	57.	10
4.	18	31.	16	58.	40
5.	2	32.	4	59.	8
6.	10	33.	100	60.	27
7.	4	34.	30	61.	7
8.	16	35.	70	62.	50
9.	81	36.	18	63.	12
10.	4	37.	80	64.	3
11.	2	38.	10	65.	10
12.	6	39.	8	66.	12
13.	42	40.	16	67.	6
14.	36	41.	5	68.	3
15.	56	42.	2	69.	4
16.	5	43.	40	70.	20
17.	10	44.	10	71.	10
18.	5	45.	7	72.	12
19.	10	46.	18	73.	5
20.	4	47.	6	74.	80
21.	3	48.	50	75.	2
22.	6	49.	10	76.	54
23.	9	50.	90	77.	40
24.	6	51.	9	78.	5
25.	72	52.	54	79.	64
26.	7	53.	9	80.	3
27.	8	54.	40		